Greater Than a T Copenhagen Denmark

50 Travel Tips from a Local

Maddie Ipsen

Order Information: To order this title please email lbrenenc@gmail.com or visit GreaterThanATourist.com. A bulk discount can be provided.

Lock Haven, PA
All rights reserved.
ISBN: 9781521977309

>TOURIST

Maddie Ipsen

BOOK DESCRIPTION

Are you excited about planning your next trip? Do you want to try something new while traveling? Would you like some guidance from a local? If you answered yes to any of these questions, then this book is just for you.

Greater Than A Tourist Copenhagen by Maddie Ipsen offers the inside scope on Copenhagen, Denmark. Most travel books tell you how to travel like a tourist. Although there's nothing wrong with that, as a part of the Greater than a Tourist series, this book will give you travel tips from someone who lives at your next travel destination.

In these pages you'll discover local advice that will help you throughout your stay. This book will not tell you exact addresses or store hours but instead will give you an excitement and knowledge from a local that you may not find in other smaller print travel books. Travel like a local. Slow down, stay in one place, and get to know the people and the culture of a place.

By the time you finish this book, you will be eager and prepared to travel to your next destination.

Maddie Ipsen

TABLE OF CONTENTS

BOOK DESCRIPTION

TABLE OF CONTENTS

DEDICATION

FROM THE PUBLISHER

WELCOME TO > TOURIST

INTRODUCTION

1. Why Visit Copenhagen?

2. When To Visit

3. Where To Stay

4. Getting Around

5. What To Bring

6. Learn Basic Phrases

7. Staying Safe

8. Rent A Bike

9. Living With A Host Family

10. Skål & Tak For Mad

11. Danes And Privacy

12. Meeting Danes

13. Making Friends On Tinder

14. Jump In The Harbor

15. Living In A Folkehøjskole

16. Dressing Like A Dane

17. Experiencing Hygge

18. Danish Festivals

19. Studying In Copenhagen

20. View Local Theater

21. Speaking English (Or Other Languages)

22. See Nyhavn and The Little Mermaid

23. Going Out

24. Eat At Papirøen

25. Eating Traditional Danish Food

26. Eating In Denmark – Vegetarian Edition

27. Shop At Torvehallerne

28. Grocery Shopping On A Budget

29. Drinking In Copenhagen

30. Taking In The Coffee Culture

31. Sweet Treats

32. Christiania

33. View Modern Art At The Louisiana Museum

34. Explore Art At Glyptoteket

35. Relax In The Botanical Gardens

36. Stroll Through Roseborghave

37. Amager Strandpark

38. Walk The Royal Tour Of Copenhagen

39. Walk Along The Lakes

40. Ride A Boat Taxi

41. Shopping Streets

42. See The City From The Round Tower

43. Kastellet

44. Copenhagen For Kids

45. Take A Day Trip To Kronborg

46. Dance In Fælledparken

47. Paying In A Cashless City

48. Seeing Strollers Outside

49. Danish Traditions

50. Tipping And Taxes

Top Reasons to Book This Trip

WHERE WILL YOU TRAVEL TO NEXT?

Our Story

Notes

DEDICATION

This book is dedicated to both of my families. To my American parents who gave me the opportunity to study abroad and to my Danish family who took me into their home and gave me an unforgettable experience.

Maddie Ipsen

ABOUT THE AUTHOR

Maddie is a student who lives in Wisconsin, but it soon moving to Austria. Maddie loves to play music and listen to Podcasts. Maddie loves to travel…

I spent four months living with a host family in Copenhagen, Denmark. Specifically I lived in Østerbro, one of the neighborhoods just outside the downtown area. Although I attended an American university, I spent a lot of time engaging in Danish cultural activities with my host family and exploring the city on my own.

Maddie Ipsen

HOW TO USE THIS BOOK

This book was written by someone who has lived in an area for over three months. The author has made the best suggestions based on their own experiences in the area. Please check that these places are still available before traveling to the area. The goal of this book is to help travelers either dream or experience different locations by providing opinions from a local.

Maddie Ipsen

FROM THE PUBLISHER

Traveling can be one of the most important moments in a person's life. The memories that you have of anticipating going somewhere new or getting to travel are some of the best. As a publisher of the Greater Than a Tourist book series, as well as the popular 50 Things to Know book series, we strive to help you learn about new places, spark your imagination, and inspire you.

Thought this book you will find something for every traveler. Wherever you are and whatever you do I wish you safe fun, and inspiring travel.

Lisa Rusczyk Ed. D.
CZYK Publishing

Maddie Ipsen

WELCOME TO > TOURIST

Maddie Ipsen

INTRODUCTION

As of writing this in June 2017, I've been back from Denmark for over a year and I'm still talking about how important it is to me. In some ways it's difficult for me to explain just why this city means so much to me, but in other ways I could go on for hours. For right now, I'll limit it to 50 tips.

Maddie Ipsen

1. Why Visit Copenhagen?

Copenhagen is a unique city. There is a blend of the historical and the modern in a way that doesn't feel jarring. Sankt Peders Bageri, the oldest bakery in Copenhagen, fits in perfectly down the block from The Living Room, a local 50's inspired bar. The museums display both modern and historical art to show the progression of the artistic process.

But if I were to truly talk about what I miss, it's the people and the culture. I was welcomed into a home as I lived with a host family who gave me first-hand experience as to what it's like to live like a Dane. Whether it's the culture of *hygge*, loosely translated as "coziness," or standing completely silent in the train on my way to class, the culture was one that felt so easy to slip into.

In short, I would recommend visiting Copenhagen to see a city focused on conserving the environment to improve its future as well as preserve and restore its past. While you're there, there's a good chance that you'll meet some incredibly warm people with a culture that's just different enough that you'll be able to explore your perspective on your own culture.

2. When To Visit

I spent a spring semester in Copenhagen from January through May. The bright side? The weather got nicer as the semester went on. Copenhagen is always beautiful, but the best time to visit would be between April through September because the flowers are in full bloom. While I was there, I learned that the cemeteries are more than just cemeteries; they are beautiful parks. If you're willing to take a trip outside Indre Byen (the city center), take time to visit Bispebjerg Cemetery in northern Copenhagen. The sakura trees blossom in April and turn the entire park a beautiful shade of light pink.

Because Copenhagen is on an island, the weather is never too extreme. Being from Wisconsin, I appreciated a winter that wasn't -20° degrees Fahrenheit. If you choose to visit during the winter, the temperature never dropped below 25 degrees and the snow melted by the next day. In fact, when I showed my host sister a picture of my home university in Wisconsin, she told me that it looked like the movie "Frozen." The spring and summer weather stays roughly around 60-75 degrees. In short, the weather in Copenhagen is temperate year-round and the best time to visit would be from March through August.

3. Where To Stay

While Copenhagen is fairly well-known for being an expensive city, there are options to find cheap places to stay when you visit! A good friend of mine stayed in the Generator Hostel when she visited me. Shared rooms (mixed, 1-8 guests) start around $19 per night. When I asked my friend, this was her experience: "They had a full bar and restaurant with tons of seating. They had free WiFi, a huge outdoor terrace and like 5-6 floors of rooms. It's super close to Nørreport and they have a ton of amenities that they list on their website… Good service, felt very safe! I would recommend staying in smaller rooms with fewer people if they can afford it [if you'll be going out a lot]."

You could also stay at the Copenhagen Backpackers Hostel has rooms starting at $15. The location is great, it is about a block away from Tivoli. Like the Generator Hostel, the Backpackers Hostel also has free WiFi, a bar, and breakfast. The Backpackers Hostel is a lot smaller than the Generator Hostel with only 38 beds. Because of this, it is important to book as soon as you can.

I would also highly recommend staying in an Airbnb. My parents stayed in one when they visited me and had a fantastic experience. Staying in an Airbnb is a great way to live in a Danish house and get to know the neighborhoods. They will most certainly be more expensive than staying in a hostel, but are likely cheaper and more authentic than most hotels.

4. Getting Around

First we should cover how Copenhagen's transportation is set up. The main part of the city is in Zone 1. The zones move outwards the further you get out of the main city. For example, the university where I studied was in Zone 1 (only a block or two away from the capitol building), but I lived in Zone 2. The Copenhagen airport is in Zone 4, and you will be able to buy a transportation pass for the first four zones.

I had a transportation pass that gave me unlimited access to any public transportation within the first two zones of the city. There is another type of transportation card that you can use to pay for what you use.

Buses: The bus system in Copenhagen is incredibly efficient and easy to manage! Like with any city, the key is making sure that you get on the bus going in the right direction.

Subways: There are two main subway trains in Copenhagen which are clearly diagramed in the stations. It is especially important to check which subway you're taking when going to the airport! Although they merge when going in the opposite direction, only one subway will take you to the airport.

Trains: The trains are more complicated than the subways, although they are also extremely efficient. These are mostly used when you will be traveling outside of the city or to the outer parts of Copenhagen.

5. What To Bring

One of my favorite things about Copenhagen is that the weather is very temperate because the city is on an island. When I arrived in January, there was no snow and the temperature was much warmer than what I had just left in Wisconsin.

I would suggest bringing a jacket for the days when it gets colder. To truly fit in like a local, make sure it's black – this is a solid rule of thumb for anything you wear in Denmark. I would also recommend bringing tennis shoes (another Danish core part of Danish fashion) that you can comfortably wear to walk around the city.

Although you can buy them in Copenhagen, I would suggest buying outlet adapters before you leave. They will be much more expensive if you buy them in Copenhagen. The adapter that you will need for Denmark is universal for the majority of Europe – England's is different if you decide to travel there. My favorite type was the one that had both adapters and USB chargers. There are plenty of banks that will exchange U.S. Dollars for Danish kroner with a low exchange rate which would be lower than drawing money from international ATMs.

6. Learn Basic Phrases

The advice I received was simple: "Speak as though you have a potato in your mouth."

Basic Rules

"J" = Y

"Hv" (questions words, i.e. hvor, hvem) = V

Consonants are soft

"V" when not "hv" = silent

Ø = Say the "ee" sound, but shape your mouth like you're saying "O"

Å = "O," but in the back of the mouth

Y = say the "ee" sound, but shape your mouth like you're saying "oo"

A few phrases

Hello, my name is… = Hej, jeg hedder (Hi, yai heller)

"Hej" is very informal. Substitutes:

Goddag (Goh-day) = Hello

Godmorgen (Goh-morgen) = good morning

Godaften (Goh-aften) = good afternoon or evening

Where is…? = Hvor er…? (Vor er...?)

How are you? = Hvordan går det? (Vor-den gaar det?)

7. Staying Safe

At one point, I told my mom "I feel safer in Copenhagen at 3 in the morning than I did in Chicago while walking home from work." Copenhagen is an incredibly safe city, but like any city it is important to use common sense. Keep an eye on your belongings at all times, especially on public transportation. Almost every place will use credit or debit card anyway, so there isn't a reason to carry large amounts of cash on you. One of the easiest ways to stay safe is to simply act like a Dane; when you're walking around the city, just keep to yourself.

When you go out, I would highly recommend going with friends. I almost never went out by myself unless I was going out for coffee before or between my classes. Simply be smart, use common sense, and you'll be completely fine. In case of emergency, dial (+45) 112.

8. Rent A Bike

Arguably the best way to experience Copenhagen like a local is to ride a bike through the city. As a warning: Danes can be fairly aggressive while on their bikes. This was always strange to me because I would always have very nice interactions with Danes and then they would almost run you over while on their bike.

Bike rental places are located all over Copenhagen, but two of the biggest bike rental shops are Bycyklen and Baisikeli. Bycyklen bikes are electric rental bikes that you'll find in most big cities. Just look for the white bikes with tablets. Conversely, Baisikeli is a shop that focuses on donating profits to African countries and making health care more accessible in rural areas. Although it is less convenient, it is focused on using the proceeds for good causes.

Perhaps most convenient, Donkey Republic allows you book a bike from your phone. Because you won't always have mobile data or WiFi, the bike rental is based on Bluetooth usage. All you need to remember is which of the twenty stations you used to rent the bike when you bring it back.

9. Living With A Host Family

I cannot express enough how much I loved living with a host family when I studied abroad in Denmark. If you are studying in Copenhagen, especially if you're at The Danish Institute of Study Abroad (DIS), I think that living with a host family is one of the best choices. Because DIS is an American study abroad university, living with a Danish family was a great way to experience the culture in a way that I wouldn't have if I was living with other American students.

From my first night, my host family gave me a truly Danish experience. I arrived in Copenhagen the night of my host sisters' shared birthday party and spent the entire night meeting the family and experiencing the culture. Part of the Danish culture is that they keep to themselves unless they have a reason to talk to someone. My extended host family had no problem talking to me because they knew that I was part of the family now. It helps that I was the fifth student to stay with my host parents and the extended family members were used to it.

When staying with a host family, it is important to make an effort to be part of the family. Some easy ways to do this are to cook, go on bike rides, or go shopping with them. One thing that I found particularly beneficial was to study in a very central space so that I could still be involved with them while I was studying.

10. Skål & Tak For Mad

One of the first things I learned when I was living with my host family was to say "Tak for mad" after every meal. This translates into "Thank you for the food," and it's simply a way to thank the chef for the work that the put into preparing the meal. This is more relevant to eating dinner at home with family or friends rather than eating at a restaurant. This phrase is also used to symbolize the end of a meal. In Danish dinners, no one leaves the table until everyone is finished eating (although children may also be excused early). Once everyone is done, they all say "Tak for mad," and clean up their dishes.

When visiting Danes for dinner, it is usually customary to bring something for them to thank them for hosting you. Wine is the most typical gift for hosts, although feel free to bring other drinks or appetizers as you see fit.

Danish meals, especially those which include alcoholic beverages, are typically started out with the word "Skål!" This is simply the Danish word for "Cheers!" If you have the opportunity to go to a Danish celebration, such as a birthday party or wedding reception, "skål" is something you'll find yourself saying a lot. When I attended a Danish confirmation party, I learned to simply say this word when I wasn't sure what was going on (as long as the other people around me were also saying it).

Maddie Ipsen

"Life itself is the most wonderful fairy tale." Hans Christian Andersen

Maddie Ipsen

11. Danes And Privacy

Remember one thing when you're trying to meet Danes in Copenhagen: They're not rude, they're just private people. This was actually great for me because it meant that people weren't randomly approaching me on the street while I was simply trying to walk from the train station to my class. Copenhagen is an introvert's dream city.

What this means for people visiting Denmark is that you shouldn't assume that people will be as outgoing as if you were visiting, for example, the Midwest. Don't be afraid to ask people for directions, though, because they aren't at all unfriendly. Danish culture simply has established that it is important to give people space. I experienced a bit of culture shock when I came back and a stranger at the gym asked me how my workout was going.

A big part of this can be seen in one simple question that we may use as a greeting: "How are you?" For Americans, that's almost an extension of "hello," without necessarily requiring an answer. In Denmark, and most European countries, asking "how are you" is another way of saying "Give me an in depth explanation of how you're feeling, and I'd also love to hear about your day." So if you don't want to seem like a tourist, maybe don't approach a random Dane on the street and ask "Hey, how are you?"

12. Meeting Danes

One of the first, and perhaps most important, things I learned about Danish culture was that Danes are very private people. It is not uncommon to walk through a silent street during the day. Don't be afraid to ask people for directions if you are looking for something, but you will definitely give yourself away as a tourist if you smile and wave at people on the street.

But don't let that discourage you! There are many ways to meet and befriend Danes. One of the ways that I found was to attend the "Language Café" at Studenterhuset where I could meet native Danish speakers and befriend other people who were trying to learn the language. Fredagbar (Friday Bar) is also a great way to meet people; simply go to a bar around 4:00 or 5:00 p.m. to meet people who have just finished work or school. A personal favorite of mine was the Bastard Café, a board game bar located about 15 minutes away by foot from Nørreport train station. There are free board games (as well as those that you have to pay for) and drinks. There was not a single time I went there in which it wasn't completely filled with people.

In short, Danes are very private people, but you can meet Danes if you make an effort to go out and meet people. All that is really involved is going out and doing things that you're interested in, and you'll be sure to meet Danes who are interested in doing the same things.

13. Making Friends On Tinder

Tinder in the U.S. is primarily used to meet people that you might want a romantic relationship with, which is exactly why I was more than a little surprised when my friend told me that her host parents suggested that she download the app to make friends in Copenhagen. Do whatever makes you feel comfortable, but Tinder has a different connotation in Denmark than it does in the States. If you feel so inclined, using this app can be an easy and convenient ways to make friends who can show you how to truly experience the city like a local.

14. Jump In The Harbor

If you've heard of the Polar Plunge, this idea won't sound too strange to you. There is a Danish tradition of jumping into one of the many harbors of Copenhagen. My professor explained it to us through the lens of the history of vikings from Denmark. Jumping in the harbor was a way to show strength, especially if it was done during the winter.

If jumping into the harbor in the middle of Copenhagen is a little extreme, as it is for me, you can also visit the Islands Brygge Harbour Bath. This is a little bit more removed from the central part of the city, but it is still a great way to spend a summer day and see the city skyline. Although it's nothing extravagant, it is an exciting way to experience Danish traditions.

15. Living In A Folkehøjskole

A *folkehøjskole* was first described to me as "something like a liberal arts school," but while talking to one of my friends I learned that it was much more than that. This is essentially a living and learning community for students who have graduated from gymnasium (high school) but aren't entirely sure what they want to study in university.

My friend described to me that the students can take classes at a *folkehøjskole* to develop skills and learn about what they want to pursue. It also offers regular social events, nightly dinners, and an opportunity to learn about Danish traditions. The students in a *folkehøjskole* are typically between 19-25 years old.

There are different types of *folkehøjskoles* including ones that focus on spirituality, sports, and youth schools (for ages 16-19). However, if you choose to study in Copenhagen and live in one of these schools, you will be living on the outside of the city. This means the commute will be longer than if you were living in the city, but the train system is very fast and efficient.

16. Dressing Like A Dane

When in doubt, wear black.

I was told before I left that the Danes always look great and are very fashion-forward. Once I was there, I realized just how true that was but that the Danish look is actually incredibly easy. Gather up some basics (pants, shirts, or dresses with no patterns) in all black and don't be afraid to layer. The goal is to be comfortable - because we are in the country of *hygge* - while looking good. The typical footwear is a pair of neutral colored sneakers.

The easiest way to stand out in Denmark is to wear bright colors, so the best way to not look like a tourist is to gather up as many dark colored clothes as you can find. Minimalism is also a big part of Danish culture that is reflected in the fashion. Accessories are not worn very often, and when they are they are typically very small. Needless to say that statement necklaces are not very common.

17. Experiencing Hygge

Before I went to Copenhagen, I had never heard of "hygge" or any of its variations. However, this is a very important part of Danish culture. Recently it has spread to American culture, including articles in The New Yorker and being added to the Oxford Dictionary.

A very rough translation is "coziness," although there's a lot more that goes into it than you might expect. For me, it was the nightly dinners with my host family. My dad said that "hygge" for him was sitting out by a fireplace with our dog. "Hygge" really depends on the person's preferences and what is most comfortable for them. As my Danish professor explained, there are a few basic rules for experiencing "hygge:" (1) hygge cannot be experienced alone, (2) candles are typically involved, and (3) it is completely subjective.

"Hygge" may be difficult to understand at first because Americans live in a culture in which we are constantly rushing from one thing to the next, but "hygge" is an essential part of Danish culture that may be hard to understand until you truly experience it. And the best way to do that is to visit Copenhagen and live like a local.

18. Danish Festivals

Tivoli is open all year round, but it is especially known for its holiday events during the winter. Starting in November, there is a "Crazy Christmas Cabaret" every day as well as performances in the theater. The gardens truly light up in the winter to celebrate the holiday season.

The current monarch of Denmark is Queen Margrethe II who celebrates her birthday on April 16. This is a national holiday in Denmark, so be sure to drop by Amalienborg Palace at noon to see the queen and the soldiers' salute to her.

Copenhagen Carnival takes place on Whitsun (50 days after Easter) for three days in Fælledparken. This isn't entirely Danish as it is a Brazilian-style festival, but it is still a must-see for anyone visiting Copenhagen during the summer. As the festival draws closer, the events will be shared on the website. Sankt Hans Aften takes place on the summer solstice (June 23) to celebrate the longest day of the year. It is a night filled with bonfires and celebrations of the shortest night of the year.

19. Studying In Copenhagen

If you're an American student who has the opportunity to study abroad, I would highly recommend studying at the Danish Institute of Study Abroad (DIS). As the name would suggest, the university is dedicated to study abroad students. As a psychology student, I had so many options available to me. I was so excited for all of the courses that were available; it was a great way to experience Danish culture by studying with professors from Copenhagen and look at what I had learned from a different perspective. Being a DIS student also meant that I got discounts for most of the restaurants and cafes in the area of the university.

That being said, DIS is an American university and your classes will be filled with other American students. For musicians, I would highly recommend auditioning for the Royal Danish Academy of Music (RDAM). There are musicians from all around the world who are completely dedicated to improving themselves. It's a fantastic way to meet other musicians while also making friends from different cultures.

Otherwise, applying to Copenhagen University is an option to study with Danish and other international students. The only risk with this is that the classes will most likely be taught in Danish. It's a good idea to check the website for Erasmus students to try to find classes that are taught in English.

20. View Local Theater

If you ever receive the chance to see a show at the Royal Danish Opera, take it without hesitation. It is one of the primary architectural draws to the city as five of the fourteen floors are under water. The building is strikingly beautiful from the inside and out; it can be seen across the water from Amalienborg palace. Tickets for the shows typically range from $23 to $140.

The Royal Danish Playhouse is another option if opera isn't for you. The large building overlooks the water and contains three stages. While you're waiting for the show, or simply dropping in during the day, you can stop at the cafe or cocktail bar.

The oldest public theater in Denmark is Folketeatret on Nørregade. There are shows available for everyone including a children's stage. The website has all of the upcoming shows, but it is in Danish so be prepared to use Translate.

Maddie Ipsen

"The world is a book, and those who do not travel read only a page." Saint Augustine

Maddie Ipsen

21. Speaking English (Or Other Languages)

The national language of Denmark is, believe it or not, Danish. However, the Danish language is not very universally spoken so all adults have been speaking English for years. I know that I was nervous because my Danish was very basic (and I was told I sounded German when I tried to speak Danish), but every person I met was willing to switch to English when we spoke together. This is generalizable to any place you go; even the small, local places that probably don't see a lot of tourism had people who were willing to switch to English. Let's face it: Danish is a difficult language that is extremely different from English.

If you happen to speak other languages, there's a good chance you'll be able to use those in Copenhagen as well. Children can choose to learn either German or French when they are in fifth grade. Because of this, both of these (more widely spoken) languages are very common around the city. Being able to read German is very helpful when reading Danish because the words are similar, although they sound very different.

22. See Nyhavn and The Little Mermaid

Two of the most famous places in Copenhagen are Nyhavn and The Little Mermaid. Nyhavn is the series of colorful buildings that you will see in the most popular pictures of the city. There are a lot of shops around this area, although they are very based in tourism. This isn't a place in which locals visit very often, however the Christmas market makes it a great place to visit during the winter. It is also worth visiting Nyhavn 20 to see the former home of Hans Christian Andersen. However, one of the good parts about this tourist spot is that there are plenty of great places to visit along the canal such as an amber shop and a small ice cream shop. While you're at Nyhavn, don't forget to jump on the trampolines by the harbor!

The Little Mermaid is another tourist attraction that is the inspiration of many souvenirs. Be warned: the statue itself is much smaller than you might expect. In 2013 it turned 100 years old and is still one of the biggest draws to Copenhagen. This statue is more representative of Hans Christian Andersen's portrayal of the little mermaid who stared longingly out to the sea and later became part of the sea foam. The statue is in the neighborhood Østerbro, which is where I lived when I was there. It's a beautiful neighborhood with a lot of different restaurants and cafés.

23. Going Out

There is probably little to no surprise that Studenterhuset, my favorite coffee shop/bar, was also one of my favorite places to go with my friends. At the end of the second week of my semester, Studenterhuset held a party for all the exchange and study abroad students. I'm not sure if they hold this every year, but I certainly hope they do because it was one of the best experiences I had. They gave out free Tuborg (local Danish beer) for the first two hours of the party and played great music.

Bastard Café is a board game café/bar that is located fifteen minutes by foot from Nørreport station. It's more expensive than Studenterhuset, but there are many free board games that you can play. They also have more drink options, specifically cocktails, than Studenterhuset. This is a perfect place if you want to have a calmer night than you would at a club.

As I found, it is entirely possible to simply stumble upon a party when you're walking through the city. When my friends and I were on our way to Bastard Café, we saw bright lights and heard loud music coming from 7-11; when we approached we learned that they were holding a party to celebrate the release of a new cider. So don't be afraid to simply wander the city and see what you happen upon.

24. Eat At Papirøen

Literally translating to "the paper island," Papirøen is an indoor food truck market. According to the Visit Copenhagen website, this name came from the fact that the building used to house the Procurement Association of the Danish Press. If you don't want to eat inside, you can take your stuff outside and eat on the harbor where you can look across the water at the Royal Danish Opera. The indoor kids' playground called Experimentarium is right next door, so there is a great option for everyone in the family.

While Papirøen can seem very intimidating because it is a large hall that is filled from wall-to-wall with food stands, there are so many great options and it's a great place to go if you have a lot of time to kill. The website has a list of all of the stalls and vendors so you can get an idea of what is available. It's a very quick walk from both Christianhavn and Nyhavn, so you could easily spend a day walking through both historic neighborhoods and stop in for lunch.

25. Eating Traditional Danish Food

One of the things that you definitely need to try when you visit Copenhagen is *smørrebrød*, a Danish open-faced sandwich. It is most often served on dark rye bread with different types of meat or seafood. There are various *pølser* (hot dog) stands located around Copenhagen. Breakfast is a good time to try *æbleskiver*, apple pancakes served with sugar and jam. All of these can be found at almost any Danish restaurant. Schønnemann is a traditional Danish restaurant which specializes in *smørrebrød*.

Don't be surprised if Danes ask you to pronounce *rød grød med fløde*, a Danish dessert of red berries in sauce and topped with whipped cream. This is a very common dessert that can be found most restaurants. Maybe just don't try to pronounce it if your order it and would like to be understood.

My parents' favorite restaurant when they visited was Cafe Klimt, a cheaper restaurant in central Copenhagen which features the art of Austrian painter Gustav Klimt. If you go at lunch, there will be multiple options for traditional food, such as a delicious salmon dish.

26. Eating In Denmark – Vegetarian Edition

I'll admit, I was a little scared about what I would eat when I was planning on going to Copenhagen. As a vegetarian with an allergy to shellfish, I was worried that I wouldn't be able to find anything to eat.

Copenhagen is an incredibly vegetarian-friendly city! Like most cities, a lot of the restaurants display their menus outside. Even if they don't, it's very easy to check online! Here is a list of a few of my favorite places with vegetarian options.

If you're in the mood for American food, Max Hamburger feels like a throwback restaurant, but one of those that has order kiosks in the front for those times when you don't want to interact with people. The first time I went there was when my vegan friend visited me and we passed the restaurant and saw that they have four different types of veggie burgers. I was sure I must have imagined it until we sat down and had completely different meals. For a more gourmet option, you can also visit Halifax Trianglen in Østerbro (a northeastern neighborhood in Copenhagen). Like the millennial that I am, I waited until my parents were visiting to go to the really nice place.

RizRaz is a completely vegetarian, Mediterranean inspired buffet. I almost cried when my class went there for lunch and I realized I could eat everything that was offered there.

27. Shop At Torvehallerne

One could easily spend hours walking through Torvehallerne and looking at the different foods available. There are two buildings which are completely filled with delicious foods from Copenhagen and across Europe. Located across from Nørreport Metro station, Torvehallerne is very central in Copenhagen. Admittedly, it's not very cheap so this is best saved for when you want to splurge on nice food.

There are options available from imported wine, locally baked goods, and various meats and seafood. In addition, there is are coffee shops and benches where you can rest or bring the coffee with you while you shop. There is a small area with picnic benches outside the buildings, so you may sit down and eat a meal if you want. My personal favorite was Sweet Valentine, a small bakery that also sells sandwiches including vegetarian options. Smag Torvehallerne is a great place to grab food to-go. Although I never paid much attention to the meat options that are available, there are many butchers who are selling very fresh products. I also really enjoyed the stations that sold local and imported wine and beer. I don't remember the names of either of the places, but keep an eye out because they may be hard to find.

28. Grocery Shopping On A Budget

Netto is a good chain of grocery stores around Copenhagen. I always remember it based on the yellow sign with the dog. The stores are generally pretty big and have a wide range of products. ALDI is also an option that you might be more familiar with that has multiple locations around the city. Irma costs a little bit more than Netto, but also has a great selection with plenty of options.

Be prepared to bag your own groceries. It was something that I had not even considered until I went shopping with my host dad and he asked why I wasn't helping put away the food. Oops. Simply because it's better for the environment, I would suggest bringing your own recyclable bag to pack your groceries. Some stores may also ask you to pay for the bag; if you don't have one, you can buy one at the store.

29. Drinking In Copenhagen

The two most common Danish beers that you'll find are Tuborg and Carlsberg. While you can't tour the Tuborg factory, you can take a cheap tour of the Carlsberg brewery which is located within the main city area of Copenhagen.

If you go between June and August, check out the *hyggeligt* Friday Bar at the Carlsberg brewery from 4 p.m. to 10 p.m. Friday Bar (fredagbar) is a part of the Danish culture in which you gather with your friends and/or coworkers to go to a bar after work. It takes place at any bar you want to visit!

The Carlsberg brewery also offers tours which provides 1 beer or soft drink as well as 1 gift for adults ($15) and students ($11). Kids may also take the tour and receive 1 soft drink and gift. More information is available at the Visit Carlsberg website!

For students, I would highly recommend Studenterhuset. Denmark is fairly expensive, especially bars, but Studenterhuset provides very cheap drinks for students who provide ID from their university. In addition to wine, beer, and cider, Studenterhuset will also make mixed drinks. Parties are held here about once a month; you can check the schedule by visiting their website.

30. Taking In The Coffee Culture

I was not a coffee drinker before I went abroad, but coffee is so much part of the culture that it's almost impossible not to drink it. Unlike in the United States, where we tend to take our coffee on-the-go for quick caffeine, the Danes drink their coffee slowly to truly enjoy the flavors and experience of drinking it with others. One important thing to know before you go is that most places sell their coffee in glasses rather than mugs or travel cups.

A few of my favorite places to gather with my friends and family are The Donut Shop, Baresso, and Riccos. All three have free WiFi! To this day, The Donut Shop is my favorite latte. Part of it is because I was running late for class with a migraine and they gave me a free shot of vanilla in my latte (thank you!!), but the coffee is delicious and the little shop is one of my favorite places to spend my time. It offers a discount for students when they order the donut and latte special, about $4.50 for students and $7 for non-students. The people who work there are so nice and happy to speak in English because they work close to the study abroad university.

Baresso is a chain that I usually visited with my host family. It is because of Baresso that I started drinking coffee; my host dad and I got there after my host mom and sisters to find that my host mom had ordered a drink that she thought I would like. Riccos' coffee and sweets are delicious. Like Baresso, Riccos is a chain with multiple locations around Copenhagen.

Maddie Ipsen

"The traveler sees what he sees, the tourist sees what he has come to see."
Gilbert K. Chesterson

Maddie Ipsen

31. Sweet Treats

In one of my classes we asked our professor where to get the best pastries and her answer surprised us: 7-11. While they aren't bad at all - and are, in fact, very convenient - they weren't my favorites.

One of my favorite places, which I recommend to every single person who goes to Copenhagen, is Sankt Peders Bageri. I went on Tuesdays to grab a vegetarian focaccia, but it is especially busy on Wednesdays for their $1.50 cinnamon rolls that are the size of your face. I learned the hard way that they do not take international debit/credit cards, so be sure to bring cash with you!

The Donut Shop is a tiny little shop located very close to the study abroad university. As a note for students: they provide discounts! My personal favorite was the "Donutella," but it was perfectly paired with their amazing coffee.

In addition, I think any student would enjoy Studenterhuset. This is a student run cafe/bar in Copenhagen which has delicious sweets during the day. During the spring or summer, you can find delicious ice cream places around Copenhagen as well. My favorite was the one in a plaza near Studenterhuset. This one is a cart that comes once the weather is nicer. If you're visiting Nyhavn, you can also visit Vaffelbageren for delicious homemade ice cream and eat it while walking along the canals.

32. Christiania

Christiania is one of the most interesting places in Copenhagen with a rich history. Christiania was started as an independent city within the larger city of Copenhagen in protest of the lack of affordable housing in Copenhagen.

Christiania is easily distinguished by the large tree mural by the main entrance that is ornately decorated. Once you walk inside, there are winding sidewalks along the neighborhood. There is a very large building that hosts an art gallery with pieces made by local artists. The art is also very cheap if you want to buy something while you're there. There are also many outdoor vendors along the sidewalk where you can buy unique souvenirs and gifts that would be difficult to find anywhere else in the city. Christiania also has some of the cheapest coffee shops that you'll find within Copenhagen.

Although it is one of the most popular tourist destinations in Copenhagen, there are also very strict rules that must be upheld. They are also listed on the sign outside Pusher Street, but remember: No running, no photography, no phone calls. I made a point to keep my phone in my bag the entire time I was in Christiania, but especially when I walked past Pusher Street. This is for the safety of the visitors so that they do not run into conflict with the dealers. As long as you follow these rules, Christiania is a fun and interesting place to visit.

33. View Modern Art At The Louisiana Museum

Copenhagen is an incredibly artistic city and one of the best places to see this demonstrated is at the Louisiana Museum of Modern Art. I would suggest that this should be a day trip; it takes about half an hour to get there from central Copenhagen (as it is located in Humblebæk) and there is so much to see that it would be best to try to spend at least a few hours there.

The Louisiana Museum is open from 11 a.m. – 10 p.m. If you are able to go on a nice day, I would suggest visiting the sculpture garden outside the building. The sculptures overlook the channel of water between Denmark and Sweden. The Kusama Installation is also a must-see in the Louisiana Museum. It is a dark room with walls and the ceiling covered in mirrors and lights hanging down. The lights look like small ping-pong balls and change colors while you are in the room. There are also constantly changing temporary exhibits, so the Louisiana Museum is a great place to visit at any time.

A ticket for an adult costs 125 Danish kroner, or approximately $19.30, about $17 for students with identification, and free for museum members and children. There is also a discount if you go with a group of people.

34. Explore Art At Glyptoteket

As central as it is in Copenhagen, I stumbled upon Glyptotek completely by accident. This is the sculpture museum in Copenhagen, with art stemming from ancient Greece to modern Danish artists. Guided tours are available, although they are fairly expensive and start around $120.

I would highly recommend buying some lunch from the museum and eating it while sitting in the central area of the museum which is filled with beautiful trees and flowers, called the Winter Garden. Because the museum is so large, taking a break in the central area is a great respite.

The Glyptotek costs about $14.70 for adults over 28, $7.70 for adults age 18-27, and is free for people under 18. It is also free on Tuesdays. It is open from 11 a.m. – 6 p.m. from Tuesday through Sunday, 11 a.m. – 10 p.m. on Thursdays, and is closed on Mondays.

The permanent exhibits include art and sculptures from Egypt, Denmark, ancient Greece and Rome, and France. One of their most famous permanent exhibits is of the art made by Edgar Degas. This art explores using art to show the many different ways that the body can move by using human and dog models.

35. Relax In The Botanical Gardens

A great place to visit for free is the Botanic Gardens (or Botaniskehave) located in central Copenhagen. The multiple buildings are built with glass to provide natural lighting for both the plants and the guests. There are many different areas of the garden that allow plants from many different climates to grow throughout the year. Take your time, because the gardens are huge and cover a lot more space than you would think at first glance. Don't be afraid to also stop in either of the cafés to take a break and enjoy drinking coffee in a beautiful garden.

The Botanic Gardens are easy to miss; they're behind a brick wall by Copenhagen University and it's easy to think that they're simply part of the university. From April through September, the gardens are open from 8:30 a.m. – 6:00 p.m. and from 8:30 a.m. – 4:00 p.m. from October through March.

36. Stroll Through Roseborghave

Rosenborghave, or called King's Garden in English, is a beautiful spot that attracts people during the spring and summer. The sidewalks are lined with tall, uniform trees. The central line of these trees leads to one of the two famous statues of Hans Christian Andersen. This is a great place to go if you want to have a picnic or take a nice walk through the city. It isn't unusual to walk through the garden during the spring or summer and see people studying or playing outside.

This space has something for everyone. During the summer, musicians will play here for the Copenhagen Jazz Festival. There are also puppet shows held for children during the summertime. This is the time in which the flowers, which cover most of the garden, are in full bloom.

The gardens are also surrounded by some very historical buildings such as the Hercules Pavilion, which is now used as a cafe after previously being used by King Christian V for royal dinners. The Commandant's House is also located next to the gardens and hosts special exhibits.

37. Amager Strandpark

My favorite place in Copenhagen is Amager (pronounced Ah-mah) Strandpark. My friend and I visited as a day trip and were struck by the beautiful beach and the famous windmills in the distance. It's perfect for a nice bike ride or run along the coast. Take the M1 train on the subway system to the Amager stop. You'll be able to see the beach park from the stop and can easily walk there by walking east down Italiensvej.

During the summer, you can participate in many different activities such as kayaking or windsurfing. There are various food stands along the path, or you can take a walk up the hill to an abandoned military fortress. Walk a little bit further and you'll find a restaurant to stop if you want to take a break from the hike. In my opinion, a trip to Amager Strandpark is a great way to spend a day during the summer. Even in colder weather, which is when I went, there is so much to see and do. My friend and I hiked up the large hill to find that a military fortress had been built underneath it. There are also a lot of cafes and restaurants in this area if the weather isn't as nice when you visit. During the winter, you can go skiing at the environmentally-friendly waste-based energy plant. It is the only place in Copenhagen where you can do this. I never went, but my host parents told me that it is a great experience that truly demonstrates the way in which Copenhagen is dedicated to protecting the environment.

38. Walk The Royal Tour Of Copenhagen

Christiansborg is a beautiful building with a rich history. The movie, *A Royal Affair*, explores one of the most infamous affairs in Danish history. Here's a brief summary: the relationship between the young queen of Denmark (Caroline Mathilde) and the royal advisor (Johan Struensee) influenced Danish culture and laws. There is still a lot to see in the building, which is wrapped around a courtyard. One of the places that my class visited is the hall which features the different carriages that have been used by the royal family throughout the years. You can also see the ruins under Christiansborg of the castles that have burned down. Walking through the ruins, which have been turned into a museum, is a great way to have an interactive experience with Danish history.

Rosenborg is home to the crown jewels of Denmark as well as portraits of Caroline Mathilde and Johan Struensee. There is a beautiful garden outside which hosts many students during the spring and summer. When you walk along a long line of trees, you will find yourself facing one of the two statues of author Hans Christian Andersen.

Amalienborg is home to the Danish royal family and was built after Christiansborg burned down. There are four palaces which house the different members of the royal family. Once an hour, you can watch the changing of the guard outside the palace.

39. Walk Along The Lakes

The lakes that run through Copenhagen are absolutely stunning. If you have time between places that you need to go, I would highly recommend taking a stroll by the lakes. I lived at the far northern edge of the lakes and was able to walk to both universities I attended by walking along the lakes. Each of the lakes, which are separated by man-made divisions, are lined with cafes and restaurants. Be careful of the swans that swim in the lakes. If you're a runner, this is a great route with a perimeter of 3.85 miles (or 6.2 kilometers).

This is a great way to take time to relax or get to know the city better simply by walking along the water. But the lakes also serve an ecological purpose; Copenhagen is particularly susceptible to cloudbursts, but these lakes serve to hold the flood water that come from cloudbursts. Once again, Copenhagen architects combine aesthetics with functionality to create beautiful lakes that keep the city's ecology strong and healthy.

40. Ride A Boat Taxi

During my first week at my university, the faculty had us take a walking tour of the city. When we got to the end, we realized that it would be faster to go back if we took a boat taxi. Because most of central Copenhagen is focused around the harbors, traveling through the water is a great way to see a lot of the city. If you have a transportation pass, you are free to take any of the boat taxis.

The boat taxis will take you through all of the main areas of Copenhagen including Nyhavn and Christianshavn. There is truly so much to see that is located around the harbors, the best way to see this city.

Maddie Ipsen

"To travel is to discover that everyone is wrong about other countries." Aldous Huxley

Maddie Ipsen

41. Shopping Streets

The two main shopping streets in Copenhagen are Strøget and Købmagergade. Strøget is the main, very large one which stretches over half a mile. The shops range from little souvenir shops to Louis Vuitton. This is a very tourist heavy area in Copenhagen, but the shops are very unique from each other and it's definitely the best place to go to shop.

Købmagergade is another shopping street which intersects with Strøget. This one is also visited very often by tourists as it is host to Rundetårn. Købmagergade has more chain stores, including two locations of H&M and a bookstore; this street is likely geared more towards students. Both of these pedestrian streets are located in downtown Copenhagen and are great for both tourists and locals to go shopping.

42. See The City From The Round Tower

Rundetårn (the Round Tower) was built in the 1600's as one of the multiple projects of King Christian IV. A lot of the famous architecture in Copenhagen was established during this period because Christian IV was dedicated to expanding the cultural heritage of Denmark. The Round Tower was first built as an observatory, but is now a very famous tourist attraction both for the beautiful church that is attached to it and the famous ramp that leads to the top. Instead of having a stairwell, a spiraling ramp was built so that horses could take the king to the top of the tower. While that isn't the case anymore, it certainly makes the hike to the observation deck a lot easier.

Once you get to the top, the observation deck looks out upon the historical downtown part of the city. The fee for adults is only $4 and less than $1 for children (ages 5-15). While you walk up, there is also an exhibition hall for art as well as a library that was used by Hans Christian Andersen.

43. Kastellet

Kastellet, or the Citadel, is another historical part of the city that was established by King Christian IV. It was initially a military fortress that was built next to the harbor, it is now used as a park that leads to The Little Mermaid statue. It is located in the neighborhood of Østerbro, which meant that it was a 10-minute walk from where I lived. For me, it was one of the best kept secrets in this part of the city. While most of the tourists flocked to The Little Mermaid, I was happier walking through the barracks and along the water that surrounded them.

In order to get to Kastellet, all you really have to do is get off the commuter train at Østerport station and walk towards The Little Mermaid. I'm incredibly biased because I lived in this neighborhood, but it is absolutely beautiful. I would highly recommend walking through the multiple gardens around the train station after exploring Kastellet.

Outside, but very close to, Kastellet is a small English church called St. Alban's. It's much smaller than most of the churches in Copenhagen, but the architecture is still beautiful.

44. Copenhagen For Kids

Legos are easily one of the most famous things to come out of Copenhagen. The LEGO store is located on the middle of the shopping street Strøget in central Copenhagen. The "living room" area is a way to give the kids time to play while the parents take a break from walking around the city.

Tivoli is a short walk away down Strøget. The gardens are absolutely beautiful, but there is also a theme park for the kids. There are also events every day for both the parents and children. The prices depend on when you go, but, for example, an unlimited ride ticket costs about $35 including a ticket for the child and for the adult co-rider.

I would also highly recommend the Hans Christian Andersen Museum. It's easy to miss, but look out for Ripley's Believe it Or Not because it is right next door. I went when a few of my friends visited me; the museum is beautiful and interactive. It is truly perfect for the entire family. It displays a few of Andersen's most famous fairy tales including Thumbelina, The Emperor's New Clothes, and - of course - The Little Mermaid. The stories are read to you (you can choose English, Danish, or German) or you can read the cards that are next to the displays.

45. Take A Day Trip To Kronborg

If you're in Copenhagen for more than four or five days, I would highly recommend taking a day trip to Kronborg Slot - better known as the Hamlet castle, Elsinore. It is about an hour and a half out of Copenhagen by train and located in the town Helsingør.

The castle is absolutely stunning; you have to pay to go in, but you can explore the entire castle down to the dungeons underneath. It's difficult to do justice to the beautiful architecture and paintings in Kronborg. You can take a self-guided tour around the castle, which wraps around the courtyard. The dungeons are dark and creepy, but I would definitely suggest exploring them (ideally with someone else). While you're down in the dungeons you can see Holger, the sleeping king. The myth is that the king sleeps until Denmark is in danger and will wake to protect his country. It's definitely a creepy and awe-inspiring sight.

While you're up in Helsingør, you can stop at the tiny restaurant outside of the castle to eat traditional Danish foods. You can also see southern Sweden and visit if you feel like taking a ferry ride across the channel.

46. Dance In Fælledparken

Fælledparken is a large park in Østerbro which hosts a large dance program for five weeks in the summer every year. There are free dance lessons for beginners from Monday through Thursday as well as open dance each evening starting at 10 p.m. Sundays is also Family Dance so every generation of the family can join. There are different types of dance taught every day and everyone of any skill level is encouraged to come. The website (sommerdans.dk) shows the full program for the summer including the types of dance being taught, the skill level, and the schedule for family dances.

47. Paying In A Cashless City

There is very little reason to withdraw a lot of money while in Copenhagen. Almost any place you visit will accept credit or debit cards as long as you have the international chip. The only place I can think of that didn't was Sankt Peders Bageri, which was probably a good thing because it forced me to reduce the amount that I went there.

I thought this was actually pretty convenient because otherwise you would be holding onto a lot of currency that you wouldn't use outside of this country. The average exchange rate is that 10 Danish kroner is equal to $1.50, so things may seem incredibly expensive but really aren't that bad. Although Copenhagen has a reputation for being expensive, I'd say it's about the same as any big city.

Although I never personally used it, a lot of places in Copenhagen are also moving toward mobile pay. The MobilePay app was actually developed by the bank of Denmark, Danske Bank. Whatever your app of choice is, this can actually be an even easier way to pay while in Copenhagen. That being said, credit or debit cards are more likely to be used than mobile payment.

48. Seeing Strollers Outside

One of the most disconcerting things that I saw when I got to Copenhagen was that people would leave strollers, with the children in them, outside of restaurants. When my class asked our professor about this, she said that it was simply part of the culture. It is believed that children will sleep better and grow up to be healthier if they sleep outside in the fresh air. Denmark is a remarkably ecologically friendly country, so it makes sense that the citizens would want their children to grow up and be influenced by the fresh air. The safety issue is what was so stark to all of us American students, but Copenhagen is a ridiculously safe city. While it is something that I don't understand, it is a part of the Danish culture so don't be too shocked if you see children unattended; their parents are just inside and watching them.

49. Danish Traditions

For an incredibly secular country, many religious holidays and traditions are celebrated in Denmark. There are a few that are also celebrated in America (Valentine's Day, Easter, Christmas, etc.), but there are some that I wasn't familiar with before I went.

For example, Fastelavn is a holiday that takes place right before Catholic Lent. This holiday is very similar to Halloween in that children dress up and ask for candy. Rather than throwing eggs at houses, there is a tradition of lightly hitting your parents with a twig which supposedly originates as a fertility ritual. Great Prayer Day is also celebrated on the Friday after Easter Sunday.

While it might have only had to do with my host family and their friends, but Confirmation was also a very important tradition. We watched the confirmation ceremony at the church and then followed the family to the party afterwards. My host mom told me that confirmation parties often feel like wedding receptions with lots of toasts and dancing. If you befriend a family whose child is being confirmed, it's definitely a fun way to experience the culture.

50. Tipping And Taxes

When you go out to eat or buy something, what you see is what you pay. The taxes are included in the price that is listed. This makes it incredibly convenient when you are budgeting how much you want to spend while you are in Copenhagen. It is also relevant for any place that you would go; there are no added taxes in restaurants, bars, or stores.

Tipping also isn't as commonplace as it is in the United States. In Copenhagen, servers are typically paid a living wage and therefore don't rely on tips for their income. Of course there are places in which tipping is encouraged, but it is not as strongly enforced as it is here. In the States it is normal to pay at least 15% for good service, but it's much more normal in Copenhagen to pay whatever change you have as the tip. If you're getting over culture shock and forgot to give a tip, don't worry about it. It's completely normal and already covered by their pay. I would definitely suggest tipping places where the service is above and beyond and definitely places in which there is a tip jar on the counter.

Maddie Ipsen

Top Reasons to Book This Trip

- **Coffee**: Denmark's coffee culture got me hooked
- **Food**: Both the traditional and vegetarian food is amazing
- **Modern and Historical Culture**: blending for a fantastic experience

Maddie Ipsen

> TOURIST

GREATER THAN A TOURIST

Visit GreaterThanATourist.com
http://GreaterThanATourist.com

Sign up for the Greater Than a Tourist
Newsletter
http://eepurl.com/cxspyf

Follow us on Facebook:
https://www.facebook.com/GreaterThanATourist

Follow us on Pinterest:
http://pinterest.com/GreaterThanATourist

Follow us on Instagram:
http://Instagram.com/GreaterThanATourist

Maddie Ipsen

> TOURIST

GREATER THAN A TOURIST

Please leave your honest review of this book on Amazon and Goodreads. Thank you.

We appreciate your positive and negative feedback as we try to provide tourist guidance in their next trip from a local.

> TOURIST

GREATER THAN A TOURIST

You can find Greater Than a Tourist books on Amazon.

Maddie Ipsen

> TOURIST

GREATER THAN A TOURIST

WHERE WILL YOU TRAVEL TO NEXT?

Maddie Ipsen

> TOURIST

GREATER THAN A TOURIST

Our Story

Traveling is a passion of this series creator. She studied abroad in college, and for their honeymoon Lisa and her husband toured Europe. During her travels to Malta, an older man tried to give her some advice based on his own experience living on the island since he was a young boy. She thought he was just trying to sell her something. When traveling to some places she was wary to talk to locals because she was afraid that they weren't being genuine. She created this book series to give you as a tourist an inside view on the place you are exploring and the ability to learn what locals would like to tell tourist. A topic that they are very passionate about.

Maddie Ipsen

> TOURIST

GREATER THAN A TOURIST

Notes